GEARED FOR GROWTH BIBLE STUDIES

THE MAN
GOD CHOSE

A STUDY IN THE LIFE OF JACOB

BIBLE STUDIES TO IMPACT THE LIVES
OF ORDINARY PEOPLE

Written by Dorothy Russell

The Word Worldwide

CHRISTIAN FOCUS

For details of our titles visit us on our website
www.christianfocus.com

ISBN 1-84550-025-3

Copyright © WEC International

10 9 8 7 6 5 4 3 2 1

Published in 2005 by
Christian Focus Publications Ltd, Geanies House,
Fearn, Tain, Ross-shire, IV20 ITW, Scotland
and
WEC International, Bulstrode, Oxford Road,
Gerrards Cross, Bucks, SL9 8SZ

Cover design by Alister MacInnes

Printed and bound by Bell & Bain, Glasgow

CONTENTS

QUESTIONS AND NOTES

ANSWER GUIDE

PREFACE

GEARED FOR GROWTH

'Where there's LIFE there's GROWTH:
Where there's GROWTH there's LIFE.'

WHY GROW a study group?

Because as we study the Bible and share together we can

* learn to combat loneliness, depression, staleness, frustration, and other problems
* get to understand and love each other
* become responsive to the Holy Spirit's dealing and obedient to God's Word

and that's GROWTH.

How do you GROW a study group?

* Just start by asking a friend to join you and then aim at expanding your group.
* Study the set portions daily (they are brief and easy: no catches).
* Meet once a week to discuss what you find.
* Befriend others, both Christians and non-Christians, and work away together

see how it GROWS!

WHEN you GROW ...

This will happen at school, at home, at work, at play, in your youth group, your student fellowship, women's meetings, mid-week meetings, churches and communities,

you'll be REACHING THROUGH TEACHING.

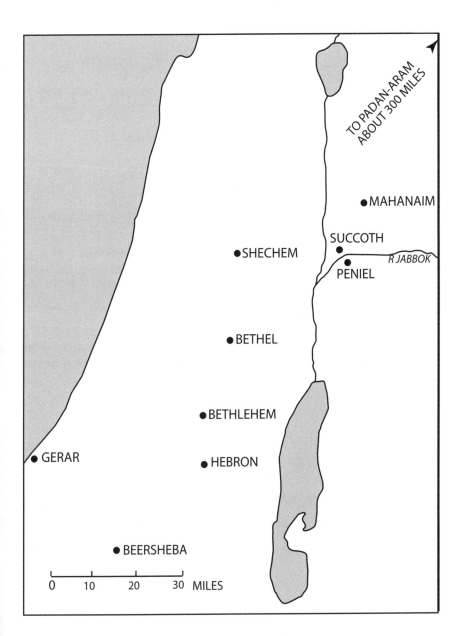

TO PADAN-ARAM
ABOUT 300 MILES

● MAHANAIM

SUCCOTH
●
● SHECHEM

● PENIEL

R JABBOK

● BETHEL

● BETHLEHEM

● GERAR

● HEBRON

● BEERSHEBA

0   10   20   30   MILES

JACOB . . . .

5

INTRODUCTORY STUDY

When reading a biography, we are often introduced first to the parents and even the grandparents of the person concerned. So let us have a look at Jacob's ancestral Family Tree.

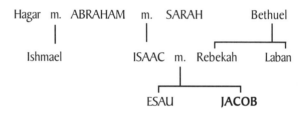

Hagar m. ABRAHAM m. SARAH   Bethuel

Ishmael   ISAAC m. Rebekah   Laban

ESAU   JACOB

ABRAHAM was living in the city of Ur, a vast civilization, when God said to him:
'Leave your native land, your relatives and your father's home, and go to a country that I am going to show you. I will make of you a great nation, and through you all the nations of the earth will be blessed."

ISAAC lived all his life in the land of Canaan. God told him:
'Live here, and I will be with you and bless you. I am going to give all this territory to you and your descendants. I will keep the promise I made to your father Abraham.'

JACOB was visited by God in a dream. God said:
'I will give to you and your descendants this land on which you are lying. And through you and your descendants I will bless all nations.'

* * *

What can you discover about God from the following verses?

Exodus 3:6; Exodus 3:15 and 16; Luke 20:37 and 38; Acts 3:13

Now let's see what we can find out about Abraham, Isaac and Jacob. What kind of men were they?
Each of you should now look up one of these references, read it to yourself and then share anything you have discovered about what Abraham was like.

Genesis 12:1-4; 12:10-13; 13:8-9; 13:18; 18:1-5; Hebrews 11:11; Genesis 22:1-3; 22:10-12

Now do the same for Isaac.

Genesis 22:6-9; 24:62-67; 25:19-21; 25:27-28; 26:12-13; 26:19-22

Are we getting some idea of the characters of these two men? Does it surprise you that God was willing to be known as their God?

But what about Jacob?
Let's try this quiz and see how much we know about him.

What does his name mean?
What were the two incidents where he cheated his twin brother?
What did he have to do then?
What was 'Jacob's ladder'?
Whom did he fall in love with at his uncle's place?
How did his uncle cheat him?
How did Jacob later get the better of his uncle?
How many sons did Jacob have?
Which one was sold as a slave into Egypt?
What did his other sons tell him had happened?
Where did Jacob end his days?

Does it surprise you that God was willing to be known as 'the God of Jacob'?
In Hebrews II, that great chapter about men of FAITH, we read: 'Therefore God is not ashamed to be called their God'.
He allows Himself to be called 'the God of Abraham, Isaac and Jacob'. Can you say with the Psalmist:

'This God is our God for ever and ever,
He will lead us for all time to come' (Ps. 48:14)?

The following extract is taken from *Conversations with Jacob*, by William H. Pape.

He was limping when I first met him, and I instinctively distrusted him. He had a crooked, twisted smile and furtive eyes. He was going my way, however; and as we walked together he began to tell me of his grandfather, for whom he had the greatest admiration. He told story after story about the old gentleman, each more amazing than the first.
'Left everything he did,' explained the stranger with the crooked smile, 'and went off to look for a city designed and built by God.'

'I remember, too,' he added, 'my father telling me about the day Grandfather took him on a three-day trip to Mount Moriah to give him up as an offering to God. A man of faith, he was, extraordinary faith. It's not really surprising that God enjoyed my grandfather and even began to call Himself the "God of Abraham".'

Then my friend stopped abruptly and turned to look me full in the face. His eye was no longer furtive, and his smile was certainly more pleasant. He began to speak quickly, and with a surprising frankness.

'But I'm no Abraham. I'm just not in his class,' he said. 'I never could do the kind of things he did. All my life – well, nearly all my life – I've been plagued with fear and bothered with doubts.'

Without realizing what I was doing, I looked at his lame leg and began wondering if his physical handicap had been the cause of all his troubles. It was easy to visualize him as a cringing little boy surrounded by bullying tormentors. I was embarrassed to find that his eyes had followed mine and that he'd guessed my thoughts. He laughed.

'No,' he said. 'I haven't limped all my life. That's not why I've had such troubles with my fears.'

'Then maybe you lacked a mother's love, or suffered from an elder brother,' I suggested.

'You're wrong again,' he answered with much amusement.

'I am a twin, and I had an affectionate mother. I really don't know how I came to be the kind of man I was. All I know is that I moved cautiously and tried to figure things out in advance. I liked to handle my own affairs my way. But unfortunately, I had a nagging fear that I wasn't quite smart enough to handle all my problems.'

'No one ever guessed that, of course. And I pretended to myself that it wasn't true. But let me tell you a most remarkable thing. God is my God too! He even went so far as to call Himself the God of Isaac (that's my father) and the God of Jacob (that's me). Extraordinary! You'd never think that God would have any time for a man like me, would you?'

He continued his limping walk, and with a little hesitancy I asked him how he came to be that way.

'I don't want to embarrass you,' I said, 'but ... what happened to your leg?'

(To be continued)

> God has one single aim as he directs the life of the man He has chosen – that is, that he should be conformed to the image of His Son.

(Look out for the *words in the box* each week. They will help you to see what *God* is doing.)

STUDY 1
GOD'S CHOICE

QUESTIONS

DAY 1   *Genesis 24:1-4, 10-27, 61-67.*
(If you are not familiar with the story, read the whole chapter).
a) How did God show Abraham's servant that the girl at the well was the one He had chosen to be Isaac's wife?

b) Look at the Family Tree again. How were Laban and Bethuel related to Rebekah?

DAY 2   *Genesis 25:19-26.*
a) What did Isaac pray to the Lord about?

b) What did Rebekah ask the Lord about?

c) How long were they married before they had any children?

DAY 3   *Psalm 105:5-6, Romans 9:10-16, Galatians 1:15.*
a) When did God choose Jacob for Himself?

b) What can you discover about the reason for God's choice?

DAY 4   *Joshua 24:2-4.*
a) Where was Abraham when God chose him?

QUESTIONS (contd.)

Genesis 17:17; 25:7-9, 26.
b) Here's some arithmetic for you to do! How old were the twins, Jacob and Esau, when their grandfather died?

DAY 5   *Genesis 25:27-34.*
a) In what ways did the twins differ from one another?

b) How does Hebrews 12:16-17 show that Esau was not a suitable man to carry on the line of promise?

DAY 6   *Genesis 26:1-16.*
a) This is the first recorded time that God spoke to Isaac. What was the message He gave him?

b) When the people of that area (Philistines) became jealous of Isaac's wealth, what did they do?

DAY 7   *Genesis 26:16-35.*
Look at the map on page 5 to find Gerar and Beersheba.
a) How did God gradually move Isaac and all his possessions back to Beersheba, where He wanted him?

b) What did God do at Beersheba?

c) What did Isaac do?

NOTES

God first chose Abraham, one man, to be the father of a great nation, God's people.
But something seemed to go wrong! Abraham reached the age of 100, and his wife 90, and still they had no child.

When, humanly speaking, there was no hope, God moved into the situation, and miraculously gave them a son.
Isaac grew up among the Canaanite people. But wait a minute! The heir to God's promise must have a God-fearing wife, and all the local girls were idol-worshippers. Here was another impossible situation.

But God had already chosen a wife for Isaac, and He wonderfully led Abraham's servant to the right girl.
Now the line of ancestors for God's chosen people could continue. But year after year went by – 17, 18, 19 years, and it looked as though Rebekah couldn't have any children. What now?

In answer to Isaac's prayers, God allowed Rebekah to become pregnant. And she got double what she expected!
Esau was born first, but God said, 'I have chosen Jacob to be the spiritual leader. From him shall come my nation.'

Was there some mistake? Surely God knew that the firstborn must inherit the birthright.

* * *

We are not told much about Jacob as a boy or a young man, except that he was Mother's favourite and spent his time around home, in contrast to his twin brother who was a real outdoor man. No doubt Jacob avidly drank in the stories about God calling Abraham from another country, and giving him the covenant promise – to make a great nation. And the exciting tales of how the line of promise was passed on through Isaac his father, and how through him all nations of the world would one day be blessed.

There must have been a longing in Jacob's heart to be the one to carry on this line – a longing which grew ever more intense as the years went by. Yet Esau was the firstborn; carefree, happy-go-lucky Esau who cared nothing for ancient traditions.

How frustrating for Jacob! Can you imagine him growing to maturity, and continuing year after year with this desire eating into his soul? How helpless he must have felt! Was there no way that he could gain for himself the position he desired above all else? He must have heard about the prophecy given at his birth, but that seemed like an old wives' tale, and nothing had come of it.

And then suddenly, one day he had his chance....

No, there are no mistakes in God's plan. He knows what He will do, if only we will be patient and not try to force His hand. God is never taken by surprise, and even when we become impatient and try to accomplish His purposes by our own methods, He overrules. Of course, we shall find that we must suffer the consequences – as Jacob had to.

When you accept Jesus Christ, and give your life to Him, you realize that you have not chosen Him – but he has chosen you! From that moment on, God will work out His plan for your life, and you just need to keep close to Him and be alert to obey.

Let's learn from Abraham, Isaac and Jacob that we don't need to fuss and worry if things aren't going the way we expect. Let's not be so presumptuous as to think we know better than God. And when our circumstances seem impossible, let's have the courage to wait, to hang on in faith, and really believe that nothing is too hard for the Lord.

> *God has told your mother, Jacob, that you the younger son, will inherit the birthright. But Jacob, why couldn't you wait? God is well pleased that you wanted the birthright so much, but He is not pleased that you got it by deceit.*

STUDY 2

SOWING AND REAPING

QUESTIONS

DAY 1   *Genesis 27:1-45.* Read the story right through today.
(The Living Bible records it most dramatically in the form of a play).
a) Why do you think Rebekah and Jacob didn't ask God's help as they made their plans?

b) Why do you think God didn't stop them doing what they did?

DAY 2   *Genesis 25:19-23; 27:1-4.*
a) Why is it strange that Isaac should have told Esau he would give him the blessing?

b) What was it that made Isaac love Esau better than Jacob? (See Gen. 25:28).

DAY 3   *Genesis 27:5-17.*
a) Imagine how busy Rebekah was that day! Make a list of all the things she did.

b) How do you think the quotation in Romans 3:8 applies to Rebekah? (LB inaccurate here).

DAY 4   *Genesis 27:18-29; Proverbs 6:17; Ephesians 4:25.*
a) What lies did Jacob tell?

QUESTIONS (contd.)

b) How do the five senses – sight, touch, hearing, taste and smell – come into this story?

DAY 5 *Genesis 27:30-40; Hebrews 12:16, 17.*
a) Who do you feel most sorry for – Isaac or Esau?

b) Why was Isaac so violently distressed when he realized he had given the blessing to Jacob?

c) What did Esau try to do when he realized what had happened?

DAY 6 *Genesis 27:41-46; 28:1-5.*
a) What excuse did Rebekah find for sending Jacob away from home?

b) Where was Jacob told to go? (See map page 5).

DAY 7 *Genesis 26:34,35; 27:46; 28:6-9.*
a) What can you find out about Esau from these verses?

b) What made Esau realize that his father did not approve of the Canaanite women?

NOTES

Have you ever wondered why this story is so well-known? Why it is so often included in Sunday School programmes? It has drama, certainly, and an intriguing plot. An old man is the butt of a daring gamble, and a mother's boy gets one up on the brother who always seems to have everything. The scheme is carefully planned and carried through – and it works!

Suspense runs high as the rightful heir comes in to claim his inheritance, only to find he has been cheated of it. Could anything contain more pathos and poignancy than the moment when Isaac asks, 'Who are you?' and Esau answers, 'Your elder son, Esau.'

Yet it's not only the plot that fascinates us. It is the characters themselves.

ISAAC, feeble though he was physically, had power. And he was determined to use his power to further his own ends, in spite of what God had ordained and in spite of his elder son's conduct.
Any of his kind around today?

REBEKAH was equally determined to get what she wanted, and had no qualms about scheming and lying to get it.
Sounds familiar?

JACOB, a ready accomplice in the deception, was only fearful in case he would be found out. Pretending to be what he really wasn't, he carried off his part cleverly, one lie topping another.
Human nature doesn't change, does it?

ESAU ignored the fact that he had made a deal with Jacob earlier about the birthright. He ignored the divine plan that he would serve his brother. His policy was, 'Let's get all we can while we can.' Then, like a frustrated child, he became angry and bitter and full of hate when he couldn't get what he wanted.

AND THE OUTCOME ...?

ISAAC was brought sharply into line with what God had planned, and he recognized that one cannot outwit God.

REBEKAH reaped only sorrow and separation for herself and her favourite son, for she didn't live to see him again.

JACOB   had to flee for his life from his vengeful twin brother.

ESAU   planned murder.

Let's learn three things from this story:

1) We can only accomplish God's will by God's methods. Don't run ahead of Him: just wait on Him in prayer, and be available.
2) God is sovereign, and it is futile to suppose that we can pit ourselves against Him and alter His divine purposes.
3) The Bible says, 'Be not deceived, God is not mocked; for whatever a man sows, that will he also reap' (Gal. 6:7).

> *God is silent here. But He is watching you, Jacob. He hears every lie you have been telling, and He is not surprised – only heart-broken. But He lets you go your own way. He doesn't stop you, even though He knows it will bring you all kinds of misery.*

STUDY 3

GOD INTERVENES

QUESTIONS

DAY 1   *Genesis 28:10-15.*
a) This is the first recorded time that God spoke to Jacob. What promises did He give him?

b) What do you think was the significance of the angels going up and coming down?

DAY 2   *Genesis 13:14-16; Psalm 105:8-11.*
a) Which promises that we listed yesterday were also given to Abraham?

b) Read John 1:51. How did Jesus use this part of Jacob's story as an illustration?

DAY 3   *Genesis 28:16-22.*
a) What did Jacob discover about God at Bethel? Read Psalm 139:1-12 and thank God for what you can discover about Him there.

b) How was Jacob's vow a poor expression of trust in God?

DAY 4   *Genesis 29:1-14.*
a) How do these verses show that God had His hand on Jacob's life?

QUESTIONS (contd.)

b) Compare this story with Genesis 24:10-15. What is missing in Jacob's story?

DAY 5 *Genesis 29:15-30.*
a) What can we discover about God's dealings with Jacob here?

b) How did Jacob react to Laban's trickery?

DAY 6 *Hebrews 12:5-11.*
a) For what purpose does God discipline His children? (Note: 'discipline' is more accurate than 'punish').

b) Apply these verses to your own life. Can you share with the group a time when God was disciplining you for His purposes?

DAY 7 *Genesis 29:31-35.*
a) What were the names of Leah's first four sons?

b) What can you find out about the tribe of Levi from Deuteronomy 10:8?

c) What can you find out about the tribe of Judah from Hebrews 7:13 and 14?

NOTES

Remember we saw in Study 1 that *God chose Jacob* before he was born?

God still has His hand on him, and it is now time to begin the discipline which will make him the man God wants him to be.

GOD SPEAKS in love, with not one word of rebuke or reproach for all that has gone before. He shows Jacob the plan He has for his life – a wonderful, exciting plan where God takes the initiative at every point.

> I am the Lord ...
> I will give you ...
> I will bless you ...
> I will be with you ...
> I will bring you back ...
> I will not leave you ...

What tremendous promises!

Isn't it incredible that God would choose a deceitful, lying schemer like Jacob, and shower upon him these amazing, unconditional promises?

Yet isn't God, in Christ, the same today?

To those whom He chooses, and who receive Him as Saviour and Lord, He says:

> *I am the Living One!* I am alive for evermore.
> *I will give you* eternal life.
> *I will bless you* with every spiritual blessing.
> *I will be with you* always, even to the end of the age.
> *I will bring you* to the place *I am preparing* for you.
> *I will never leave you*, nor forsake you.

GOD HAS IT ALL PLANNED

1) How fortunate that Jacob had many miles to travel alone, with the message of God fresh in his mind. Can't you imagine him going over every part of it as he went along?

2) When he came to a well somewhere towards the East, (and remember, he had no map!) how interesting it was that the men he met there were actually from Haran, and knew his uncle well!

3) And what a coincidence that Rachel should just happen to come along at that very moment!

Doesn't God do the same today?

What the world calls 'coincidence', the Christian sees as the hand of God working to accomplish His will.

GOD DISCIPLINES

Jacob's school of learning was in the home of Laban, a man who was harder, more grasping, more crooked and more cunning than Jacob himself. God's plan was to use Laban as a mirror for Jacob to see the kind of person he himself was by nature. This discipline wasn't pleasant, but it was necessary.

And God must discipline us, if we are His children. Hebrews 12:6 and 7 reads,

'Endure hardship as discipline, because the Lord disciplines those whom he loves.'

It will help if we remember that God is more concerned with our spiritual growth than with our physical comforts.

If Jacob had been put with some humble, pleasant person instead of Laban, he might have become proud and insufferable – and useless to God.

Similarly, God gives us circumstances through which He can teach us the lessons we need to learn. If you are going through a difficult time just now, pour out your heart to the Lord, and tell Him all your frustrations and anxieties. Then, think back over this study, and try to accept your circumstances as from the Lord. He can use sorrow, suffering and heartache to draw you closer to Himself, and to mould you into the kind of person He wants you to be.

> *God has spoken, Jacob. He wants you to know that He intends to lavish His love upon you in spite of your sinful nature. He has a purpose for your life, Jacob, and God's purposes never fail.*

STUDY 4
PRESSURES – TO TURN US TO GOD

QUESTIONS

DAY 1 *Genesis 30:1-21.*
a) Why was Rachel so unhappy? What did she do about it?

Look back at Genesis 29:32-34.
b) Why was Leah so unhappy? What did she think would solve her problem?

DAY 2 *Genesis 30:22-34.*
a) How was Rachel's problem solved?

b) Why did Laban not let Jacob leave?

DAY 3 *Genesis 30:35-43.*
This is a battle of wits!
a) How did Laban try to outwit Jacob?

b) What did Jacob do in return? (Look ahead to Gen. 31:10-12 to discover the source of Jacob's ideas).

DAY 4 *Genesis 31:1-21.*
a) What were the two reasons why Jacob decided to leave as soon as possible?

QUESTIONS (contd.)

b) What can we learn from these verses about God's guidance?

DAY 5 *Genesis 31:22-35.*
a) What three things was Laban so angry about?

b) How did God intervene?

DAY 6 *Genesis 31:36-42.*
a) Make a list of Jacob's grievances stated here.

b) What was his only hope during those tempestuous twenty years?

DAY 7 *Genesis 31:43-55.*
a) How did Laban react?

b) What were the conditions of the peace treaty? (vv. 49-53)

1. There is unhappiness and conflict in the home

Just imagine the set-up, and how Jacob felt in the midst of it all. Remember, the bickering, jealousy, anxiety and heartbreak was going on for six years! Rachel and Leah tried every way they could think of to satisfy their longings – except turning over their problems to God, and waiting on Him.

Think of an unhappy home you know. Could God solve the problems there?

2. Jacob is denied his freedom

Jacob's request, 'Let me go, so that I can return home', was politely but firmly refused. It was to be another six years before he could get away.

How would you have felt?

It wasn't as if Jacob had done wrong – no, his record was good and his conscience clear. It can't have been easy to go on submitting to authority, but Jacob made the best of things.

3. His boss tries to outwit him

There were no flies on Laban, and he didn't waste any time making sure that he would be the winner. Jacob would have lost out miserably – except for God. Sometimes our wonderful God surprises us by stepping into our problems even when we have forgotten to ask Him.

That is what He did with Jacob.

4. Attitudes become increasingly hostile

Isn't it hard to take the cutting attitude, the unfriendly glance, the whispering behind your back, the insinuating remarks that people make?

God allowed Jacob to go through this too, and then showed him that He was right by his side all the time, and felt all the slights and unpleasantness that were being hurled at him. Jacob was ready at last, God took over, and Jacob made a get-away.

5. He has to face an infuriated father-in-law

No more subtle whispering-behind-backs now. All the rage and fury of a man who had schemed and planned and lost, came hurtling at Jacob with full force.

How was Jacob able to stand against this?

How do you feel if someone accuses you vehemently to your face?

I think Jacob's initial calmness resulted from his complete honesty ('I was afraid'), the knowledge that God had told him to leave, and his innocence about the household gods.

6. His grievances, bottled up for twenty years, explode

Pressure, tension and self-pity can blow up so easily if we are not fully surrendered to the Lord. And all Jacob's resentments and frustrations poured out like the lava from a volcano.

But notice how God's discipline is accomplishing what He means it to. Self-control finally rises above the hot angry flow of words, and Jacob says, 'If God had not been with me ...', '... but God ...'.

Remember that the Spirit of God produces love, joy, peace, patience, kindness, goodness, faithfulness, humility ... and self control.

7. Finally, he makes a peace treaty

The pressures are letting up.

His wives are contented,
>   he is free to go back home,
>   he has considerable wealth,
>   and he is going to leave behind him all those difficult relationships.

He and Laban part good friends (at least on the surface!) and he offers a sacrifice to God, feeling, I'm sure, terribly relieved! And the pressures have certainly given him a new awareness of God.

So all his worries are over – or are they ...?

> *Because you are ready to listen, God can direct you now, Jacob. You have learned many of the hard lessons He has so patiently been teaching you, and He wants to move you into a new situation. Of course, He hasn't finished with you yet!*

STUDY 5

CORNERED – BY GOD

QUESTIONS

DAY 1   *Genesis 32:1-5.*
a) How did God strengthen Jacob for what lay ahead? (Read about a similar encouragement in 2 Kings 6:15-17).

b) Why did Jacob send messengers ahead of him to his brother Esau?

DAY 2   *Genesis 32:6, 7, 11.*
a) Why was Jacob so terrified?

b) What does Psalm 37:5-7 and Proverbs 3:5, 6 tell us to do when we are in trouble?

DAY 3   *Genesis 32:9-12.*
a) How did Jacob address God in his prayer?

b) What had he said earlier at Bethel? (Gen. 28:21) How did Jacob's prayer differ from the kind we read in Philippians 4:6 and 7?

DAY 4   *Genesis 32:13-23.*
a) After praying that God would save him, what did Jacob do?

QUESTIONS (contd.)

b) What did Sarah (some versions have 'Abraham') discover about God? (Heb. 11:11)

DAY 5 *Genesis 32:24-29.*
This part of the story may seem strange, but it is full of meaning for us.
a) Jacob was alone. What happened? (See Josh. 5:13).

b) Jacob was sure he could win. What happened then?

c) When the man said, 'Let me go', what did Jacob do?

DAY 6 *Read Genesis 32:24-29 again, and 2 Corinthians 12:7-10.*
God had something terribly important to teach Jacob, and He showed it to him on the physical level.
a) Paul also learned this lesson. What was it?

b) How could Jacob have applied this to the frightening situation he was in?

DAY 7 *Genesis 32:30-32.*
a) Why did Jacob call the place 'Peniel'? Can you picture the scene in verse 31?

b) Share with your group a time when you felt very conscious of God's presence.

NOTES

A man, a problem, and God. It was even simpler than that, for the man himself was the problem. Driven by desperation, he stood alone by the river bank. In the darkness of the night, without wife or family or friend to give him counsel, he walked up and down, determined that he would at last find a solution.

'Have you ever stopped discussing your problems and taken time to get away to some quiet place where there were no distracting sounds, and waited quietly for God to speak?' Jacob asked me.

'Yes, I have,' I told him. 'I never heard a mysterious voice from heaven, but I did see clearly the way out of my difficulties. What was your experience?'

'Strange and wonderful!' he answered. 'That night as I stood beside the Jabbok, terrified of the coming day when my meeting with Esau would inevitably take place, someone met me in the darkness and wrestled with me. I struggled with the stranger until dawn was breaking, and then, with one swift move, he touched me so that the sinew of my thighbone shrank and I felt myself helpless in his hands.'

'You mean, all this was happening and you didn't know with whom you were wrestling?' I asked Jacob with amazement. 'It was no ordinary person,' he answered. 'In the half-light of the morning I could see enough to know he was a messenger from heaven, and I hung on to him and cried out in desperation, "I will not let you go unless you bless me"'.

Jacob paused as he tugged on his beard thoughtfully. 'It's really amazing how much God can do in so little time when He begins to work on a man. As I stood exhausted by the riverbank, I understood at last that my strength had been my weakness. It wasn't just my thigh that shrank; I shrank, too, and saw myself small and mean and insignificant, compared to God the Almighty.'

'You know,' he added earnestly and speaking more quickly, 'when we see God big, and ourselves small, our problems get small too. As I told you, my number one problem was myself! And the angel who struggled with me that night had a solution.'

'Jacob,' I said impetuously, 'do you really believe that God can solve my problem?'

'I certainly do,' he answered, 'provided you are willing to take your burden to the Lord and submit to Him.'

And then I understood how it was that the man I'd met limping along the road came to have such a radiant smile.

(quoted from *Conversations with Jacob*, by W. Pape)

The pattern is the same for all of us if we want God's best for us.

1. Be alone with God
This is vital to a full understanding of ourselves. Only when we are alone with God can He show us exactly what we are like.

2. Come to the end of our own resources
We need to recognise, as Paul did, that 'nothing good lives in me, that is, in my sinful nature.' God has to teach us this somehow – it may be through the loss of wealth, health or family – but we must learn that of ourselves we cannot live lives that are pleasing to God.

3. Cling to God, our only hope
When we really see our hopelessness, our helplessness, then there is only one place to go – to Jesus. And when we cast ourselves completely on Him, He takes control and gives us a new name, a new nature. By surrendering to Him, we can have inner peace and joy whatever our circumstances are.

> *Sorry, Jacob! God had to bring this crisis into your life so that you would come to an end of yourself. Your relationship with Him is far more important than your comfort, or even your health, and apparently this was the only way God could get His message through to you.*

STUDY 6

EVERYTHING'S GOING WRONG

QUESTIONS

DAY 1 *Genesis 33:1-11.*
a) How do you think Jacob felt as he saw the 400 men approaching?

b) Why need he not have worried?

c) Do you ever worry needlessly?

d) How can we have victory over fear? (I Cor. 15:57 and Eph. 6:13).

DAY 2 *Genesis 33:12-17; Ephesians 4:25; Revelation 21:27.*
a) What lie did Jacob tell to Esau?

b) How seriously does God regard telling lies?

c) What can we do about it? (Ps. 141:3; I John 1:9)

DAY 3 *Genesis 33:17-20* (Refer to map on page 5).
a) What did Jacob do at Succoth?

b) What two things did he do at Shechem?

c) What attitude does God want Christians to take about living here on earth? (Heb. 13:14)

DAY 4 *I Samuel 15:22; John 14:15, 21.*
a) What is the answer to Samuel's question?

QUESTIONS (contd.)

b) If we love Jesus, what does He expect of us? Read some of the things He wants us to do in I Thessalonians 5:12-18 and Hebrews 13:1-5.

DAY 5 *Genesis 34:1-14; 33:19.*
a) Why were both Jacob and Leah to blame for what happened to their daughter?

b) Why were Jacob's sons so angry at Shechem wanting to marry Dinah?

c) What principle has God laid down for His people concerning marriage in 2 Corinthians 6:14-16?

DAY 6 *Genesis 34:13-29.*
a) List the crimes that Jacob's sons committed.

b) How does Jacob describe Simeon and Levi at the end of his life? (See Gen. 49:5-7).

DAY 7 *Genesis 34:30-31.*
Jacob was in a fix.
a) Why had he to get away from Shechem quickly?

b) Why could he not go back to Laban?

c) Why could he not go to Esau?

d) At last he was to discover what Peter later discovered. What was that? (John 6:67-68)

JACOB • STUDY 6 • EVERYTHING'S GOING WRONG

NOTES

Are you standing back and saying in exasperation, 'I thought the last study showed us that Jacob had let God take control of his life! What on earth is happening here? Things seem to be going from bad to worse.'

At Peniel, God did indeed give Jacob a new name, a new nature. But Jacob had to learn not to give in to the old nature, but rather to yield himself day by day to the God who was within, waiting to take control in every situation.

In Jacob, God gives us a picture of the struggle between the two natures, which takes place in every believer's life. We shall see that from this point on, Jacob learns more and more to submit to God's leading, and God continues to work in his life to make him the man He wants him to be.

In Romans 6 we read: 'Count yourselves dead to sin but alive to God in Christ Jesus. Do not let sin reign in your mortal body so that you obey its evil desires. Do not offer the parts of your body to sin, as instruments of wickedness, but rather offer yourselves to God.... For sin shall not be your master, because you are not under law, but under grace.'

* * *

Let's see what Jacob could have done to avoid all this worry and heartbreak.

FIRST, he could have staked everything on God's promise, 'I will be with you and protect you wherever you go.' Then he wouldn't have needed to worry about meeting Esau.

SECOND, he could have been honest and told the truth. Half-truths or lies are calculated to anger other people far more than the truth, when they find out.

THIRD, why didn't he go back to his father's people? We don't know, but God expressly told him to do this. And instead, he even built a house on the east side of Jordan. This section must cover a fair period of time.

FOURTH, he didn't need to camp right near the city of the people of Canaan. Didn't he remember the row there had been when Esau married foreign wives? And how he himself had been sent away so that he wouldn't get involved with the Canaanite women? Yet here he was, with ten sons of marriageable age, camping near the city, and buying land there!

FIFTH, how was it his sons had grown up so callous and cruel? Perhaps he hadn't spent time, as their father, teaching them moral values and how to keep their emotions in check. Of course, what a parent is, often speaks louder than what he says.

SIXTH, could he not have averted the mass murder by taking control of the situation instead of remaining silent? One would have thought he could at least have spoken out afterwards and shown that this horrible crime was a sin which God would not ignore. But all he said was, 'You have brought trouble on *me*'!

It is very easy to see what Jacob should have done. It's very easy to look at others round about and see what they should have done. It's sometimes possible to see what we ourselves should have done in a certain situation, to avoid calamity.

But it is not so easy, when temptation beckons us, to stand firm for what is right and not be led astray. However there is a way.

'If you live according to the sinful nature, you will die; but if *by the Spirit* you put to death the misdeeds of the body, you will live. Those who are led *by the Spirit of God* are the sons of God' (Rom. 8:13, 14).

> *God's heart is grieved, Jacob. You didn't need to be afraid of Esau. You didn't need to make a promise you weren't going to keep. And why did you disobey God?*
>
> *Now He is waiting ... waiting for you to come to Bethel.*

STUDY 7

THE TURNING POINT

DAY 1 *Genesis 35:1-4.*
a) What did God tell Jacob to do?

b) What did Jacob say about God in these verses?

c) How is Jacob different in his attitude to his family from last week's study?

DAY 2 *Genesis 35:1-4; 31:19; Joshua 24:14-16, 22, 23.*
a) What three things did Jacob tell his family to do?

b) What did he do with the foreign gods?

c) What significance has this for us?

DAY 3 *Genesis 35:5-8.*
a) How did they manage to escape from Shechem without being attacked?

b) Look up Genesis 24:59 and find out when Deborah first came into the story.

QUESTIONS (contd.)

DAY 4 *Genesis 35:9-15; 28:13-15.*
a) What promises did God make to Jacob?

b) How does God speak to you today?

DAY 5 *Genesis 35:16-21; 48:5-7.*
a) Who were Rachel's two sons? (Don't look up Gen. 30:22-24 unless you can't answer this!)

b) What did Jacob do years later, because of his great love for Rachel?

DAY 6 *Genesis 35:22-29; 49:3-4; 1 Chronicles 5:1-2.*
a) What far-reaching consequences did Reuben's sin have?

b) When was the next time Jacob saw Esau?

DAY 7 *Genesis 36:1-9.*
a) What reason is given here for Esau leaving the land of Canaan?

b) Where did he go?

c) In verse 12 we are told that Amalek was a grandson of Esau's. Look up Exodus 17:8-13 to see how Esau's descendants continued to reject God and His people.

Jacob's character seems so different in this study, and from this point on. Gone is the cheating, scheming grabber, and in his place is one who has come to realize that n*othing else matters but the will of God.*

Have you come to this turning point in your life yet? Can you honestly say: 'To me, nothing else matters but the will of God'?

Oswald Sanders, in his book *Men from God's School,* writes:

'When God has saved and apprehended a man, He pursues him with undiscourageable perseverance with the sole purpose of blessing him. He is constantly at work dealing with the 'Jacob' in every one of us.'

God tells Jacob to go to Bethel and build an altar to Him. Jacob immediately resumed his God-given responsibility as head of the household, and prepared his family for this dedication service.

As we too come to God in humility, let us remember to prepare ourselves in the same three ways:

1. Get rid of foreign gods
'My dear friends, do not believe all who claim to have the Spirit, but test them to find out if the spirit they have comes from God. For many false prophets have gone out everywhere' (I John 4:1).

2. Purify yourselves
'If we confess our sins ... He will forgive our sins and purify us from all our wrongdoing. The blood of Jesus purifies us from every sin' (I John 1:7 and 9).

3. Put on clean clothes
'Put off the old self ... and put on the new self, created to be like God in true righteousness and holiness' (Eph. 4:22 and 24).

* * *

In the book of Job, a conversation is recorded between God and Satan.

GOD: Did you notice my servant Job? There is no one on earth as faithful and as good as he is. He worships Me, and is careful not to do anything evil.

SATAN: Would Job worship You if he got nothing out of it? You have always protected him and his family and everything he owns. You bless everything he does, and You have given him enough cattle to fill the whole country. But now – suppose You take away everything he has, he will curse You to Your face!

GOD: All right, everything he has is in your power, but you must not hurt Job himself.

The story continues. Satan destroys Job's oxen, sheep and camels – all his wealth, and finally kills all his children. Then he waits expectantly for Job to curse God.

Job stands up and tears his clothes in grief. He says:

'I was born with nothing, and I will die with nothing.
The Lord gave, and now He has taken away. May His Name be praised!'

In spite of everything that had happened, Job did not sin by blaming God.

*   *   *

It was a bit like that with Jacob.

First, **Deborah** died and was buried. Deborah, who had come with his mother Rebekah, and who doubtless had nursed him as a child.

Sometime later, **Isaac** the old Patriarch died aged 180, and Jacob assumed a new responsibility as chieftain of the tribe.

When **Joseph** was sold as a slave (as we shall see next week) his brothers told Jacob that he was dead. So he went through the dreadful grief and heartbreak of losing him too.

'All to Jesus I surrender,' we sing. Do we really mean that *whatever* happens, we can accept it from the hand of our loving Heavenly Father, and say, 'May His Name be praised'?

Let us pray that each one of us will come to that turning point in our lives as Jacob did, where from that point on we shall be able to say, 'Nothing else matters but the will of God.'

> *Well, Jacob, you have now recognised God's gentle persistence in your life. There is a purpose behind everything that has happened. God's discipline has prevailed with you at last, and you have become the man God wants you to be.*

STUDY 8

GOD'S THOUGHTS: HIGHER THAN OUR THOUGHTS

QUESTIONS

DAY 1   *Genesis 37:1-11.*
a) What things are we told about JACOB in this familiar story?

b) What was the home situation like when Jacob was a boy? (See Gen. 25:28).

DAY 2   *Genesis 37:12-24.*
a) Where did Joseph's brothers set out for?

b) Why do you think Jacob was anxious about them?

c) What might have been Reuben's reasons for disagreeing with his brothers?

DAY 3   *Genesis 37:25-36; 25:7-9, 12, 18.*
a) Who were the Ishmaelites descended from?

b) How do we know that Jacob didn't suspect his sons of foul play?

c) Why was Jacob's grief so deep?

DAY 4   *John 11:32-38; 1 Thessalonians 4:13-18.*
a) What do these verses from the New Testament teach us about a Christian's attitude to the death of a loved one?

b) Can you share an experience of how God comforted you at such a time?

DAY 5 *Genesis 41:46-57; Acts 7:9-12.*
a) We pick up the story thirteen years later. What were the names of the two grandsons Jacob didn't know he had?

b) Where did the famine spread to?

DAY 6 *Genesis 12:10; 26:1, 2; 42:1-24.*
a) What did Abraham do when famine came?

b) What did Isaac do?

c) What did Jacob do?

d) How does Benjamin feature in this part of the story?

DAY 7 *Genesis 42:25-38.*
a) What was Jacob not prepared to do here?

b) How does this compare with Abraham's attitude in Genesis 22:1-3, 10-12? Read also Romans 8:32.

NOTES

Jacob was now chief of the tribe. When his father Isaac died, the privileges associated with the birthright became his. His word was now the final authority for all members of the tribe. One of his sons would inherit the promise of God to Abraham: 'Through you, all nations of the earth will be blessed.'

Since leaving his uncle at Haran, Jacob must have thought much about his successor. Normally, the eldest son would succeed his father as heir to his position and property. But Jacob had other ideas.

JACOB'S THOUGHTS

Just as he had, from the beginning, loved Rachel more than Leah, so he loved Rachel's firstborn, Joseph, more than any of his other children.

Joseph would have been taught lovingly by Rachel about the God of his fathers in his early years, this making an indelible impression on him. We assume that Jacob would have spent time with him too.

Possibly Joseph inherited some qualities from Rachel, which had endeared her to Jacob. Perhaps as his father looked at him he would glimpse his beloved one mirrored in the young face.

After Rachel's death, Jacob would be drawn even closer to the young lad, in an attempt to fill the aching void in his heart.

When Reuben committed the sin of immorality with Bilhah, Jacob readily decided that Leah's firstborn had forfeited the birthright which was due to him.

The bad reports that Joseph brought about his older brothers would have underlined in Jacob's mind the decision he was making.

Then it came out in the open. He presented Joseph with an ornamental coat (or long robe with full sleeves), which was a distinctive mark of favour, and implied that he was to be the future chief of the tribe.

When young Joseph told his dreams to the family, Jacob's reactions were mixed. While he rebuked the boy openly, he also kept thinking about the whole matter. Jacob remembered Bethel and how God spoke through dreams, and it is most likely that he saw these as a prophecy of things to come.

* * *

So everything was settled – in Jacob's mind, at least. He had made the decision regarding his heir and the Lord had graciously confirmed it.

And then ... tragedy struck!

'JOSEPH – MISSING, BELIEVED DEAD.'

Can you see why Jacob's grief was so devastating?

All his love and affection,
all his hopes for the future,
all his confidence in what he believed were God's plans, were shattered by this cruel blow. No wonder he refused to be comforted, and went on mourning for Joseph long past the usual time.

* * *

Remember the desolation of the two disciples who walked along the road to Emmaus on that first Easter Day? When asked why they were so depressed, they answered:

'Jesus of Nazareth was a prophet powerful in word and deed before God and all the people. The chief priests and our rulers handed Him over to be sentenced to death, and they crucified Him. And *we had hoped* that He was the one who was going to redeem Israel!'

Have you ever had your hopes dashed? It can be devastating, can't it? But listen to what God has to say:

'My thoughts are not your thoughts, neither are your ways My ways.
For as the heavens are higher than the earth, so are My ways higher than your ways and My thoughts than your thoughts' (Isa. 55:8-9).

For Jacob, the time was to come when he would realize that 'all things work together for good to those who love God' (Rom. 8:28). And Joseph would be able to say to his brothers, 'You meant evil against me, but God meant it for good, so that many people should be kept alive' (Gen. 50:20). And the disciples were to learn that Jesus died, 'so that through His death He might destroy him who has the power of death – that is, the devil – and deliver all those who through fear of death were subject to lifelong bondage' (Heb. 2:14).

Aren't you glad God's thoughts are higher than your thoughts?

> You can't see why God is allowing this dreadful thing to happen, Jacob, so all you can do is hang on and trust that He knows best. Just remember – God makes no mistakes.

STUDY 9

STILL ALIVE

QUESTIONS

DAY 1   *Genesis 42:38; 43:1-14.*
a) Imagine what Jacob must have been thinking during this discussion. What things influenced him to change his mind?

b) When you have an important decision to make, what influences you?

DAY 2   *Genesis 43:15; 44:17.*
a) What did even the Egyptian servant realize about Jacob, the father of these men?

b) What did Joseph want to find out about his father?

DAY 3   *Genesis 44:18-34.*
a) What information does Judah give here about Jacob?

b) What can you discover about the kind of man Judah was?

DAY 4   *Genesis 45:1-15.*
a) What was the first thing Joseph asked his brothers, after telling them who he was?

QUESTIONS (contd.)

b) What was God's purpose in allowing Jacob to experience the heartbreak of losing Joseph years earlier?

DAY 5 *Genesis 45:16-28.*
a) Just imagine the excitement in the Egyptian society circles! In what ways did Pharaoh and Joseph show their concern for Jacob?

b) Read Luke 15:11-24. How does the father in this story resemble Jacob at this stage?

DAY 6 *Genesis 46:1-7, 26-27.*
a) What indicates a change in Jacob's life since the days when he lived at Shechem?

b) What instruction did God give him? What four promises did He make to him?

DAY 7 *Genesis 46:28-34; 47:1-12.*
a) God had promised to keep Jacob's descendants together as a separate nation. Why did Pharaoh not want to absorb them into the Egyptian nation?

b) What happened twice during Jacob's audience with Pharaoh?

NOTES

What a difference it made to Joseph to know his father was still alive.

Joseph had tried hard to forget about his own people but when his brothers came the first time old longings were awakened. God must have given him the plan which he was so carefully and patiently working out. He must play these tricks on his brothers so that he might know for certain if they had wicked thoughts towards Benjamin, and if their consciences had been dulled by the passage of time.

But how long would it be before they returned?

Would they ever come back?

Would Benjamin come?

Was everything going to work out in time?

And above all – was his *father still alive?*

At the earliest opportunity he asked this question, and we can only guess at the relief it was to him to hear, 'Yes, he is alive and well.'

Did he wonder, later, if they had spoken the truth? When he said to them, 'I am Joseph,' he continued in almost the same breath, 'Is my father still alive?' What a difference it made to him to know that he was!

* * *

What a difference it made to the brothers to know Joseph was still alive.

Can you imagine it? What would their feelings have been? Shock, terror, then gradual reassurance as they realized he was not going to take immediate revenge. Astonishment and incredibility as the truth sank in. Then joy and excitement, and the feeling that nothing would ever be the same again. New vistas opened up: there was the anticipation of bringing the joyful news to their father, and an end to the worry of how they would feed their families.

* * *

What a difference it made to Jacob to know Joseph was still alive.

What a difference indeed!

His life was completely transformed. All his dearest wishes and desires were now fully satisfied.

'This is all I could ask for,' he said.

His first thoughts were to worship and praise God. Doesn't this indicate that he was in the habit of spending time with God? If he had not been, surely the unexpected news that Joseph was still alive would have knocked everything else out of his mind.

But he worshipped, and God shared His promises and His plans with him, and guided him as to what he should do next. He could now move forward, certain that he was in the centre of God's will.

Surely, as we think along these lines, we are reminded again of the Easter Story, when One who was dead became alive.

And what a difference it makes to you and me, to know that Jesus is alive.

Have you ever really been convinced that Jesus is alive today? Can you appreciate what that means for you personally? Do you realize how different life would be if Jesus were still dead?

A songwriter has put it this way:

'Because He lives, I can face tomorrow,
Because He lives, all fear is gone,
Because I know He holds the future,
And life is worth the living -
      just because He lives.'

> *You have come a long way, Jacob, not only in distance – to Egypt – but in spiritual maturity. You're on God's wavelength now, tuned in to Him. The moulding of your character and the loving discipline He has given you all your life, has prepared you to live with Him for eternity.*

STUDY 10

BLESSINGS

QUESTIONS

DAY 1   *Genesis 47:27-31.*
With verse 27, compare Genesis 27:28.
a) How did God fulfil the blessing that Isaac bestowed on Jacob many years before?

b) What was Jacob's greatest wish before he died?

DAY 2   *Genesis 48:1-6; 28:13, 14, 19.*
a) What were the two parts of the blessing that God had given Jacob at Bethel (Luz)?

b) How were Joseph's sons, Ephraim and Manasseh, to be included in the inheritance?

DAY 3   *Genesis 48:7-12.*
a) What had been the deepest sorrow of Jacob's life?

b) What had been his biggest surprise?

c) Have you had some deep sorrow or big surprise in your life? Can you share how God has blessed you through either of these situations?

QUESTIONS (contd.)

DAY 4 *Genesis 48:13-22; Hebrews 11:21.*
a) What blessings did Jacob confer on his two grandsons. (Read vv. 15 and 16 a few times. Aren't they beautiful?)

b) Which verse shows that Jacob was holding firmly to the promise God had given him at Bethel?

DAY 5 *Genesis 49:1-17; Hebrews 7:13, 14; Revelation 5:5.*
a) Why was the royal line to be established through Judah, and not any of his older brothers?

b) What great purpose did God have in mind for the tribe of Judah?

DAY 6 *Genesis 49:18-28; I Chronicles 5:1, 2.*
a) To what did Jacob attribute the fact that Joseph had successfully come through all his troubles? (v. 24)

b) What blessings did he confer on Joseph?

DAY 7 *Genesis 49:29; 50:14.*
a) Why did Jacob want to be buried in the land of Canaan?

Matthew 8:11; 22:31, 32.
b) What had Jesus to say about a believer (like Jacob) after death?

NOTES

If you were writing about Old Testament personalities who demonstrated the meaning of *faith*, which part of Jacob's life would you highlight? Think about this for a minute.

* * *

From the beginning of Jacob's life, he was motivated by an intense desire to appropriate all that God had available for him. The blessing of the first-born, and the land promised by God to Abraham and Isaac were of tremendous importance to him. Throughout his time with Laban, he never doubted that he would return to Canaan, and that through his descendants God's plan for the world would be worked out.

Now, at the end of his days on earth, God shows him that the birthright (or double portion of the inheritance in the land of Promise) was not to pass to his first-born, Reuben, but to Joseph, first-born of his beloved Rachel.

So the writer to the Hebrews, demonstrating the meaning of faith, selects the blessing of Joseph's sons as the outstanding act of Jacob's long career. His vision of God's purpose never dimmed, and he was absolutely sure that God could and would do what He had promised.

Therefore,

'he blessed each of the sons of Joseph,
bowing in worship over the head of his staff' (Heb. 11:21).

How the memory of that scene almost 100 years before must have flooded back into Jacob's mind. Old, blind Isaac had unwittingly given the blessing to the younger son. But now Jacob, although his eyesight was failing, was quite clear in what he was doing, and, inspired by God, gave Ephraim the major blessing.

A LAST GLIMPSE OF JACOB

At the end of his life,
What did Jacob do for his children and grandchildren?
– he prayed for them,
– he asked for material blessings for them,
– he asked for spiritual blessings,
– he entrusted them to God's care.

His greatest wish was that Ephraim and Manasseh would enjoy the same continual care and protection of God as he had had, even though they were living in the land of Egypt.

How do you pray for your children (if you have any)? or your grandchildren (if you have any)? Perhaps we can learn from Jacob here.

How did Jacob approach death?
– he showed no worry or fear, because he lived close to God,
– he desired to pass on what he had to others,
– he gave instructions for his burial,
– he looked back over God's blessings on his life,
– he praised God.

How does the Christian approach death?
Listen to Paul:

'The time has come for my departure. I have fought the good fight, I have finished the race, I have kept the faith. Now there is in store for me the crown of righteousness, which the Lord, the righteous Judge, will award to me on that day.... The Lord will rescue me from every evil attack and will bring me safely to His heavenly kingdom. To Him be glory for ever and ever' (2 Tim. 4:7, 8, 18).

And to King David:

'Though I walk through the valley of the shadow of death, I will fear no evil, for Thou art with me' (Ps. 23:4).

* * *

Jean Rees has written a fascinating, Bible-based novel called, *Jacob Have I Loved.* She concludes the book with this paragraph:

'As they laid their father to rest, no one thought of him as Jacob the wrestler, Jacob the supplanter, but as ISRAEL, the prince who prevailed with God. He rested in the land which, in years to come, would not be called the land of ISAAC, or even the land of ABRAHAM, great Patriarch though he was, but would, for generations to come, be known as the land of ISRAEL.'

STUDY 11

THE GOD OF JACOB

QUESTIONS

DAY 1   *Exodus 3:13-15; 4:5; Mark 12:26; Acts 7:30-32.*
a) By what name does God wish to be known?

b) Thinking back over our study, can you discover why God allowed Himself to be called, 'the God of Jacob'?

DAY 2   *2 Samuel 23:1; Psalm 24:3-6.*
a) What does our first reference tell us the God of Jacob did?

b) Considering David's sin (told in 2 Sam. 11), why might we be surprised that he wrote the words of Psalm 24?

DAY 3   *Psalm 20:1; Psalm 84:8.*
a) What do these verses tell us the God of Jacob (LB Israel) will do for His people?

b) Look back to Studies 5 and 6. On what occasion did *He* do just this for Jacob?

DAY 4   *Psalm 75:9; Psalm 81:1-5.*
a) What does the writer of Psalm 75 say about praising the God of Jacob? Do you feel this way?

QUESTIONS (contd.)

b) What is the command to us about this in Psalm 81?

DAY 5 *Psalm 76; Psalm 114.*
(Notice that in both of these psalms God is called 'the God of Jacob').
a) What feeling do you get as you read these psalms?

b) Why is God to be feared?

DAY 6 *Psalm 46.*
a) In contrast to yesterday's readings, what kind of picture does this psalm give?

b) What is the comforting refrain for His people in verses 7 and 11?

DAY 7 *Psalm 146:5; Acts 3:13.*
a) Do you really believe that Psalm 146:5 is true?

b) Why? How does the Acts reading link the Old Testament with the New?

NOTES

Who are you? What is your name? Why do we have names at all?

Names help us to identify who people are in relation to other people. A person may be known as Peter Bright, for example, because his father was Jim Bright; or Mrs Bright, because she is Peter's wife. This identification presupposes a close relationship, where one is not ashamed to own the other's name.

For God, therefore, to call Himself the God of Jacob, is something that should make us gasp with astonishment. When we read about 'the God of Jacob', we can realize that God allows Himself – holy, pure and almighty – to be identified with Jacob – the schemer, the grabber, the cheat. God and Jacob are united. But not because God made Himself mean and cheating like Jacob, but because, in some mysterious way, He made Jacob honest and righteous and true, like Himself.

Oswald Sanders, in his book *Men from God's School*, writes:

'The supreme lesson of Jacob's story is that no failure need be final. There is hope with the God of Jacob for any temperament, any disposition. No past failure puts the possibility out of reach. When God has saved and apprehended a man, He pursues him with undiscourageable perseverance, with the sole purpose of blessing him. He is constantly at work dealing with the Jacob in every one of us. He does not exclude from His royal service penitent men who have failed. God will turn the tables on the devil by lifting us from the scrap-heap and creating a wider and more fruitful ministry out of our very defeats.'

What a great God we, as Christians, have! We need to spend more time finding out what He is like. It's so easy to have our own ideas of Him, and not realize that 'our God is too small.' We have read a few things about His character this week, but there is much, much more, He has revealed Himself in His word, and through His Son, so read and re-read your Bible, asking yourself, 'What does this part teach me about my God?' Jacob knew his God intimately by the end of his life, and he had no Scriptures, no incarnation to help Him. How fortunate we are! Let's press on to know Him more every day, and discover for ourselves that – 'Happy is the man who has the God of Jacob to help him and who depends on the Lord his God.'

* * *

W. H. Griffith Thomas writes in his book, *Genesis, A Devotional Commentary*:

'The God of Jacob is a God of unwearying love, of unerring wisdom, of unfailing grace. He is our Refuge in spite of our sins, in the face of our failures, in view of our fears. And because He is all this, He asks for our unreserved surrender, our "unquestioning faith, our unflinching loyalty, our unfailing hope"; and whispers in our hearts,

> "Fear not, thou worm Jacob ...
> I will help thee, saith the Lord."

It is because God is the God of Jacob that we have such unbounded confidence in His mercy and grace, in His love and longsuffering. It tells us what grace can do for even the very worst of us.

As a man said to a clergyman not long ago,

> "I am cheered when I read the life of Jacob; for if the grace of Almighty God was able to straighten up that man, there must be some hope for me."'

STUDY 12

HOW CAN JACOB HELP ME?

QUESTIONS

After group discussion of each day's questions, read the appropriate section of the notes.

DAY 1   *Genesis 27:42-45; 28:10-17; Mark 1:35.*
a) Jacob was all alone. What happened?

b) What can we learn from the reading in Mark's gospel?

DAY 2   *Genesis 29:18-25; Matthew 21:33-45; James 1:22-24.*
a) How would Jacob have seen his own character mirrored in his uncle Laban's?

b) How can we use God's word as a mirror?

DAY 3   *Genesis 30:25-28; 31:38-41.*
Jacob was tied to a difficult situation.
a) What did he want to do? Why could he not do it?

James 1:2-5
b) What does God teach us through difficult situations we can't free ourselves from?

QUESTIONS (contd.)

DAY 4   *Genesis 32:7-11, Psalm 56:3, 4; Isaiah 41:10-14.*
a) Can you share with your group a time when you were very much afraid?

b) How would the verses from Psalms and Isaiah help you?

DAY 5   *Genesis 32:24-31.*
a) How is God's wrestling with Jacob a picture of what He does with His children spiritually?

b) What principle was Jesus teaching His disciples in John 12:24-26?

DAY 6   *Genesis 34:30.*
a) Jacob's reputation was ruined. If yours was dragged in the mud, how would you react?

Read Philippians 3:5-11.
b) What was, to Paul, the most important thing in life? Do you agree?

DAY 7   *Genesis 35:8, 16-18, 28-29; 37:34-35; John 14:1-3, 27; Revelation 21:3-4.*
The death of loved ones always brings sorrow and parting.
a) How did Jesus comfort His friends before His death?

b) In what practical ways can we comfort those who are bereaved?

NOTES

You will probably not find yourself in all the situations mentioned below, but try to grasp the spiritual principles and apply them to your own life.

1. Marilyn was a busy mother of three with little time to call her own. One day she slipped and fractured her leg. She found herself in hospital, away from everyday rush and bustle, with plenty of time to think – for a change! God showed her many things about herself and her life as she lay there, and she was later able to look back on that enforced rest as a time when she really listened to what God had to say.

2. David was attracted to the wife of one of his friends – a lovely girl. Instead of nipping this temptation in the bud, he made opportunities to deepen the friendship, and then seduced her one night when her husband was out of town. They planned to keep the whole affair quiet, but the girl discovered she was pregnant

     It was the prophet Nathan who held up the mirror of God's word in front of King David after this shameful event and when David recognised the full extent of his sin, he was heartbroken and repentant before God.

3. Jean's husband is an unbeliever, and resents her having anything to do with other Christians. She is forbidden to go to church, Bible study or fellowship meetings, and he has even torn up her Bible. Her husband rings up from work to make sure she stays at home. Jean finds life a real trial at the moment. But wonderfully, the Lord seems closer to her than ever before, and He is enabling her to be patient and unaggressive in her circumstances.

4. When Dr. Helen Roseveare was taken prisoner in the Congo rebellion, she was cruelly kicked, maltreated and beaten up by the Simba rebels. She writes, 'I was numbed with fear and pain and dread. The awful sense of being alone. Then suddenly, right there, in the worst moment God was there. No vision. No voice. I just knew it in the depth of my being. He did not stop the suffering or take away the pain; nor did He drive away the fear. Fear was there all through; but He was greater than the fear.'

5. Tim brought Jane along to Youth Group, hoping that she would become a Christian, like him. She enjoyed the games and outings, but continued to laugh at the idea of needing God in one's life. Tim was honestly asking the Lord about his future, but it took a long time for him to realize that unless he was willing to give up Jane, he could not have peace and guidance. When God touched him at this point he was finally willing to be obedient and broke off the relationship. It was hard, and it hurt, but the freedom he felt in his spirit

afterwards, made it worth the struggle.

6. As a young man, Arthur was converted to Christ and knew God was calling him to be a missionary. When he gave notice to the firm where he worked, and told his friends, the reaction was one of horrified disbelief: 'You're crazy! Look at all you're giving up – security, a good job, and the comforts of home! Who is going to provide for you, anyway?'

Today, after a lifetime of spreading the gospel in China and Japan, he can say, 'My God did indeed supply all my needs. Not one of His promises failed. I'd rather have Him for my security than anything else!'

7. Jean Rees shares this thought about death towards the end of her biography of her husband, *His Name was Tom*:

> One compensation for losing someone you love as much as I have loved Tom, is that death is a friend. I only feared death because it meant leaving him when he needed me.
>
> I had a glorious realization in the night a few days ago. I was praying, as I always do, in my waking moments, and suddenly realized that when I thought of death, it was not to be with Tom, but it was to be with Christ, which is far better – 'joy unspeakable and full of glory'. The last verse of a poem I wrote recently says:
>
> The practice of His presence here
> Makes earth grow futile, heaven near,
> And when the call to heaven will come
> Our passing will be going Home.

ANSWER GUIDE

The following pages contain an Answer Guide. It is recommended that answers to the questions be attempted before turning to this guide. It is only a guide and the answers given should not be treated as exhaustive.

GUIDE TO INTRODUCTORY STUDY

On page 2, make sure that people in your group realize that they have only to look up one reference each (unless the group is very small) and that they are not required to read it aloud, or tell the whole story of what they read, but simply to find out what the passage shows about the character of Abraham (or Isaac), e.g. Genesis 12:1-4 – He obeyed God implicitly.

You may find it helpful to have a pen and a large piece of paper to list the characteristics for all to see as you proceed.

What should emerge from these lists is that Abraham and Isaac were 'pretty good guys'. However, the quiz on Jacob is designed to show that he was by nature a cheat, a liar, and one who got his own way by unscrupulous scheming.

> QUIZ. The story of Jacob is told in Genesis chapters 25–50.
> Be quite sure you know all the answers yourself!

After the quiz, try to show your group how God chooses and accepts people, not on any merits of their own, but on the basis of their faith in Him. This needs careful preparation beforehand, and the following references will help you as you prepare: Romans 3:27-30; Romans 4:1-3, 13-25.

- God knew that behind all Jacob's meanness and crookedness there lay a genuine desire for spiritual blessings (as symbolized by the birthright); just as He knew that behind Esau's attractive exterior was a despising of such things, (cf. John 2:25).

- When God sees faith in a man, that man is justified in His sight – though he may have been the worst criminal – and then God can begin to work on him to make him what He wants him to be. (You may be able to give contemporary examples, e.g. Nicky Cruz, Doreen Irvine, etc.).

- Oswald Sanders in his book, *Men from God's School* says: 'God is the God of the difficult temperament, the God of the misfit, the God of the warped personality. He delights to begin where others have given up in despair. He has the solution for every problem of personality or temperament. If men will surrender their lives into His hands for drastic and radical treatment He will bring into play all His resources of love and grace' (see 1 Cor. 1:26-29).

(The excerpt from *Conversations with Jacob* will be continued in the notes for Study 5).

GUIDE TO STUDY 1

DAY 1 a) The servant asked God for a sign (vv. 12-14) and when God made things happen the way he had asked, he knew this was God's plan.
b) Laban was Rebekah's brother, and Bethuel her father.

DAY 2 a) He prayed that Rebekah would have a child.
b) She asked the Lord why the unborn babies were struggling so much.
c) Twenty years (see vv. 20 and 26).

DAY 3 a) Before he was born (since God is outside 'Time', His choice was made 'before the foundation of the world' Eph. 1:4).
b) It was not based on anything Jacob had done, but only on God's sovereignty and grace.

DAY 4 a) Beyond the River Euphrates.
b) Fifteen years. (Note that this must have been an impressive family event, especially as Ishmael must have come from quite a distance – see Gen. 25:6.)

DAY 5 a) **ESAU**   **JACOB**
hairy skin   smooth skin
outdoor man   home lover
father's favourite   mother's favourite
casual and carefree   serious and scheming
didn't care about the birthright   wanted the birthright

Esau is described as:
immoral and irreligious (RSV)
sexually immoral and godless (NIV)
involved in sexual sin and careless about God (LB)
b) Commentators do not agree with this point of view.
See Hebrews 12:16 which really reads in the AV and RSV, 'Lest there be any fornication or profane person, as Esau who sold ...'. Esau's failure was insincerity regarding the birthright; others have and do fail in other areas, i.e. immorality, sex, etc.

DAY 6 a) 'Stay in this land and I will bless you, and will keep the promise I made to Abraham.'
b) They filled in the wells which Abraham had dug.

DAY 7 a) Through conflict with the Philistines over wells.
b) God spoke again to Isaac and renewed the covenant or promise.
c) Isaac built an altar and worshipped God.

GUIDE TO STUDY 2

DAY 1

a) Perhaps they never thought of asking Him, perhaps they thought they were quite capable of carrying out the plan by themselves, or perhaps they knew God would not approve!

b) Because He has given man free will, i.e. man is free to act independently of God.

DAY 2

a) Because Isaac knew that God had ordained that the younger son would serve the elder.

b) He enjoyed eating the animals Esau brought home from hunting. (Theodore Epp comments: 'Esau had sold his birthright for a mess of pottage, and Isaac was now about to give away the blessing for a mess of venison.')

DAY 3

a) She cooked the meat; looked out Esau's best clothes and put them on Jacob; put the goatskins on him; baked bread.

b) She tried to accomplish God's will by doing evil things as a means to an end.

DAY 4

a) v. 19   I am your elder son Esau.
            I have done as you told me (see v. 3).
   v. 20   The Lord helped me to find the animal.
   v. 24   I am really Esau.

b) SIGHT: Isaac couldn't see.
   TOUCH: Isaac felt his arms to see if they were hairy.
   HEARING: He recognised Jacob's voice.
   TASTE: He ate the tasty food.
   SMELL: He smelt Jacob's clothes, and was convinced.

DAY 5

a) Personal.

b) Not only was he upset at having been deceived, but also he realized that he had been trying to do something completely contrary to God's expressed will.

c) He tried to reverse things, and get the blessing anyway. (*Note:* He wept for the blessing he had lost, not for the sin he had committed. 'Repentance' in some versions should refer to the fact that Isaac could not 'repent' – i.e. could not change his mind).

DAY 6   a) She told Isaac she didn't want Jacob to marry one of the girls of the country where they lived.

b) To his Uncle Laban's house in Paddan Aram (or Haran, or Mesopotamia).

DAY 7   a) He married two Hittite girls when he was forty, and these foreign wives caused a lot of trouble.

After Jacob had gone, he married a daughter of Ishmael (see Gen. 16:1-3, 11, 12).

b) When Jacob was sent to find a wife from among their own people.

GUIDE TO STUDY 3

DAY 1   a) I will give you the land.

Your descendants will be many.

Through you I will bless all nations.

I will be with you and protect you.

I will bring you back to this land.

b) This was symbolical of the two-way communication between God and man.

DAY 2   a) I will give you the land.

Your descendants will be many.

(Also in Gen. 12:3 – Through you I will bless all nations).

b) Jesus showed that He was the way of access to the Father, and He was also God's communication to men.

DAY 3   a) That God was there with him, and that He knew all about him.

b) He tried to bargain with God; thought he could use God to get the things he wanted. He was not yet ready to trust the Lord completely – are you?

DAY 4   a) God led him deliberately to his uncle's house.

b) Prayer, dependence on God for guidance.

DAY 5   a) God used 'Mrs. Bedone-by-as-you-did'!

b) Jacob had pretended to be Esau – now Leah posed as Rachel. Jacob had refused to wait for God – now he had to submit to Laban.

Jacob had not respected the rights of the firstborn – now he had to acknowledge this.

God used Laban to show Jacob himself as he really was. He agreed (v. 28) with commendable self-control, to work another seven years for Rachel.

DAY 6
a) So that we may share His holiness – i.e. become more like Him.
b) Personal.

DAY 7
a) Reuben, Simeon, Levi, Judah.
b) Levi was the priestly tribe.
c) Jesus was born a member of the tribe of Judah.

GUIDE TO STUDY 4

DAY 1
a) She had not had any children, and Leah had had four.
She gave Jacob her slave-girl to have children for her; and also bargained with Leah to get some mandrakes. (*Note*: Mandrakes were plants which were believed to produce fertility and were used as love-charms).
b) Leah knew Jacob didn't love her, but loved Rachel.
Having plenty of sons (see v. 20).

DAY 2
a) By God answering her prayer and giving her a son.
b) Because he realized God had blessed and prospered him because of Jacob, and he didn't want to lose him.

DAY 3
a) He quickly removed the speckled or spotted goats and the black sheep, and took them three days journey away.
b) Jacob selected the speckled animals, etc. and used them for breeding.
('In displaying the striped rods at breeding time, he acted on the common belief that a vivid sight during pregnancy would leave its mark on the embryo; but this is apparently quite unfounded', Tyndale Commentary.)

DAY 4
a) 1. Laban's sons were critical, jealous and hostile, and Laban himself was no longer friendly towards him.
2. God spoke to Jacob and told him to leave.
b) Personal. (Theodore Epp states three things that are necessary: (1) an inner desire, (2) the command or word of God, and (3) circumstances must make action possible.)

DAY 5
a) Jacob had fled without telling him; he had carried off his daughters; he had (as far as Laban knew) stolen his household idols.

b) God spoke to Laban in a dream and warned him not to harm Jacob.

DAY 6 a) His goods had just been searched, as if he was a thief.
He had done his job well, even bearing losses himself.
He had suffered from heat and cold and sleeplessness.
He had worked for fourteen years without pay.
b) In the following six years, Laban had repeatedly changed his wages. His only hope had been that God was protecting him.

DAY 7 a) He calmed down and agreed to let Jacob go (possibly pacified by not finding the stolen goods).
b) A pile of rocks was set up to remind them that God was watching them both, even though they were out of each other's sight. The terms of the treaty were that neither would cross that line with the intention of attacking the other.
(N.B. 'Mizpah' has often been used as a covenant of fellowship, whereas here it is obviously a covenant of separation).

GUIDE TO STUDY 5

DAY I a) God allowed him to see the angels that were around him.
b) To gain Esau's favour – see Genesis 27:41.

DAY 2 a) Because the messengers told him Esau was coming with 400 men, and Jacob thought they would attack him.
b) Trust in the Lord and wait for Him to act.

DAY 3 a) God of my grandfather Abraham and my father Isaac.
'If I return safely ... you will be *my God.*'
b) Jacob was worrying while he prayed, and obviously didn't have God's peace in his heart.

DAY 4 a) He proceeded to try to work things out for himself, and sent presents ahead to Esau to appease his anger.
b) That He keeps His promises.
(Notice that Jacob obviously didn't trust God to keep the promise of verse 12, and tried to make sure he would be safe from Esau by his own schemes).

DAY 5	a) A man came and wrestled with him.
	b) His hip was thrown out of joint.
	c) He continued to cling to him.

| **DAY 6** | a) 'When I am weak, then I am strong.' |
| | b) If he had recognized how helpless he was in the situation, and turned it over completely to God, he would have had strength to face it. |

| **DAY 7** | a) Because he said, 'I have seen God face to face.' |
| | b) Personal. |

GUIDE TO STUDY 6

DAY I	a) Terribly afraid.
	b) God had promised to protect him (Gen. 28:15).
	c) Through Jesus Christ and the armour of God.

DAY 2	a) That he would meet him in Seir (v. 14). Instead, he went to Succoth (v. 17).
	b) He regards it as sin.
	c) Pray to be enabled to speak the truth, and when we do lie, confess this as sin.

DAY 3	a) Succoth – he built a house for himself and made shelters for his cattle.
	b) Shechem – he bought some land and set up an altar.
	c) To remember that our homes here are not permanent and to look forward to our heavenly home.

| **DAY 4** | a) Obedience. |
| | b) Obedience. |

DAY 5	a) Jacob bought land and settled right beside the Canaanite city, giving opportunity for mixing with the people.
	b) Leah obviously neglected to teach her daughter not to fraternise with ungodly people. Partly because he had disgraced her but more important, because Dinah was one of God's people and Shechem was not.
	c) That it is wrong for a Christian to marry an unbeliever.

| **DAY 6** | a) Deceit (under the cloak of religion), murder, theft, taking the women and children. |

b) Violent and cruel.

DAY 7   a) Because the people of the land might attack him.
b) He had not got on with Laban.
c) He had lied to Esau.
d) The only place to run to is into God's arms.

GUIDE TO STUDY 7

DAY 1   a) Go to Bethel and build an altar to God.
b) God helped him in his time of trouble and had been with him everywhere he went.
c) He speaks with authority and points them to God.

DAY 2   a) Get rid of the foreign gods; purify themselves; put on clean clothes.
b) He buried them.
c) This shows that we are to 'bury' anything that might take God's place.

DAY 3   a) God caused the people round about to be afraid of them (See Josh. 2:9).
b) She was the servant who came with Rebekah when she was a bride.

DAY 4   a) Your name will be Israel.
You will have many children.
You will be the ancestor of kings.
I will give you and your descendants the land of Canaan.
b) Personal.

DAY 5   a) Joseph and Benjamin. (An interesting point is that in Matt. 2:16-18 Rachel is a symbol of the mothers of Bethlehem).
b) He pronounced a blessing on Joseph's two sons, and included them in the inheritance.

DAY 6   a) He lost the rights of the first-born son.
b) At their father's funeral. (*Note*: It was a more peaceful occasion than Esau had originally planned in Gen. 27:41).

DAY 7   a) Because the land could no longer support both him and Jacob and all their cattle.

JACOB • ANSWER GUIDE · · · · · ·

b) To Edom.

c) The Amalekites fought against the Israelites.

GUIDE TO STUDY 8

DAY 1 a) He continued to live in Canaan.

He heard bad reports about his older sons from Joseph.

He loved Joseph more than the others, and made him a special coat.

He was told about Joseph's second dream, and scolded Joseph for it, but he couldn't help thinking about the dream.

b) He was his mother's favourite, and Esau was his father's.

DAY 2 a) Shechem.

b) Because the people around Shechem knew what they had done there.

c) Because he was a blood relation, and because of the effect it would have on their father (v. 22).

DAY 3 a) Abraham and Sarah's slave-girl, Hagar. (The story is told in Gen. 16).

b) He immediately came to the conclusion that a wild beast had killed Joseph.

c) Joseph was his favourite son, born of his beloved Rachel.

DAY 4 a) Grief and weeping are right and natural – Jesus wept.

b) But Christians need not sorrow in the same way as those who are not Christians, because we have hope. That certain hope is that at death, those who belong to Christ go to be with Him.

DAY 5 *Leader* – you may need to make brief mention of what has been happening to Joseph, in case some may not know.

a) Manasseh and Ephraim.

b) Everywhere, including the land of Canaan.

DAY 6 a) Abraham went to Egypt. Isaac was going to go but God stopped him. Jacob had no command from the Lord to go, so he sent his sons to get food.

b) He was Jacob's last precious treasure and he refused to part with him. Joseph insisted he should be brought to Egypt – perhaps to see if his older brothers' attitudes had changed?

DAY 7 a) Let Benjamin go to Egypt.

b) He was willing to give his only son (God had told him to do this).

GUIDE TO STUDY 9

DAY 1   a) They had no more food.
The Egyptian ruler had said Benjamin was essential to their getting more corn.
Judah offered to be surety for him.
He realized God could keep Benjamin safe.
b) Personal.

DAY 2   a) That he worshipped a powerful God.
b) If he was still alive and well.

DAY 3   a) He is old, he loves the youngest son very much, the sorrow of losing Benjamin could cause his death.
b) Judah was diplomatic, considerate of his father, truthful, willing to suffer for someone else. (Remember Gen. 37:26? cf. Gen. 49:10).

DAY 4   a) 'Is my father still alive?'
b) To make sure Jacob's descendants would survive.

DAY 5   a) They urged the brothers to bring their father to Egypt to live, and sent animals, wagons, food and presents to him. Pharaoh also promised security for the future.
b) He was overjoyed to have his son 'back from the dead'.

DAY 6   a) Before taking an important step, he consulted God.
b) God told him to go to Egypt. He promised:
    1) to make his descendants a great nation there,
    2) He would be with Jacob,
    3) He would bring his descendants back to Canaan one day,
    4) Joseph would be with his father when he died.

DAY 7   a) Because they were shepherds, and the Egyptians had nothing to do with shepherds.
b) Jacob gave Pharaoh his blessing. (Note Jacob's dignity as a child of the King of Kings).

GUIDE TO STUDY 10

DAY 1 a) By giving him a land of plenty to live in.
b) That he should be buried with his forefathers in the land of Canaan.

DAY 2 a) God promised to give him many children, and also to give his descendants the land of Canaan.
b) They were to be counted as equal with Jacob's sons.

DAY 3 a) Rachel's untimely death.
b) That God allowed him to see Joseph after he had long thought him dead, and also to see his children.
c) Personal.

DAY 4 a) 1) The blessing of the God of Abraham and Isaac, the God who had led him all his life, and the angel who had saved him from harm.
2) The honour of perpetuating the names of Abraham, Isaac and Jacob.
3) The blessing of many descendants.
b) Verse 21.

DAY 5 a) The older brothers had forfeited this right by their sinful deeds.
b) Jesus was to be born as a member of the tribe of Judah (fulfilling the promise of Abraham, 'Through you shall all the families of the earth be blessed.')

DAY 6 a) To the power and strengthening of 'the Mighty God of Jacob'.
b) Blessings of rain and springs of water, corn and flowers, bounties of the everlasting hills.
(N.B. The Hebrew of these verses is apparently not clear, so different versions may have different renderings of these poetic words.)

DAY 7 a) To be with his forefathers. (Perhaps also to be in the land of Canaan in his death).
b) He is living, and will feast in the Kingdom of heaven.

GUIDE TO STUDY 11

DAY I   a) 'I AM', indicating that He is and was eternally the same. But also note verse 15: 'the God of Abraham, Isaac and Jacob, this is my name for ever.'
b) 1) because of Jacob's faith in him,
   2) to show that He never gives up in dealing with a person He has chosen, and
   3) possibly to give hope to those who fail time and again like Jacob did.
                                   (These are only suggestions).

DAY 2   a) He anointed David (or chose him) to be King.
b) Because David, without forgiveness, could not have stood before the Lord in His holy hill.
(*Leader* – bring out the significance of coming before 'the God of Jacob' (v. 6), who is a forgiving God. John Hercus, in his book, *David*, presents this in a fascinating way on pp. 88 and 89.)

DAY 3   a) Answer them (or be with them) in the day of trouble, protect them, hear their prayers.
b) Jacob's prayer in Genesis 32:9-12 was wonderfully answered when he met Esau.

DAY 4   a) That he will never finish praising Him and speaking about Him.
b) We are to praise the God of Jacob joyfully and with music.

DAY 5   a) Personal.
b) Because He is mighty and powerful, and has shown His terrible acts to those who oppose Him.

DAY 6   a) A picture of calm in the midst of storm, security and peace because we belong to God. Wording differs according to which version you have.
b) Note it is the *God of Jacob* who is our refuge.

DAY 7   a) Personal.
b) Because it is the same God who worked in the lives of Abraham, Isaac and Jacob, who glorified the Lord Jesus.

JACOB • ANSWER GUIDE • • • • • •

GUIDE TO STUDY 12

DAY 1
a) God spoke to him in a dream.
b) That Christians need to follow the example of Jesus, and take time to be alone with God.

DAY 2
a) By the fact that Laban cheated him of Rachel, and he had cheated Esau of his birthright.
b) A story from the Bible may show us our own faults, just as the Pharisees were convicted while they heard Jesus' parable. The holy life of Jesus, or the teaching of the apostles, may show us how far short we fall of what God expects.

DAY 3
a) He wanted to return home to his father.
   Because Laban wouldn't agree to his going.
b) He teaches us endurance, and dependence on Him.

DAY 4
a) Personal.
b) God's promises bring us courage, and when we throw ourselves completely on Him, He can be counted upon to work out the situation in the way He knows is best.

DAY 5
a) When we are trusting in our natural abilities, or are proud of our own achievements, God can weaken the self-life (by failure, consciousness of sin, etc.) so that we become dependent on Him.
b) That if we are willing to put to death the desires of our sinful selves, then God will be able to use us.

DAY 6
a) Personal.
b) To gain Christ and be completely united with Him.

DAY 7
a) He assured them of a life after death, where He would be until they were ready to go there too. He also promised them His peace in their sorrow.
b) Personal. (Include assurance from God's Word, e.g. I Thess. 4:13-18).

Christian Focus Publications

publishes books for all ages

Our mission statement –

STAYING FAITHFUL

In dependence upon God we seek to help make His infallible word, the Bible, relevant. Our aim is to ensure that the Lord Jesus Christ is presented as the only hope to obtain forgiveness of sin, live a useful life and look forward to heaven with Him.

REACHING OUT

Christ's last command requires us to reach out to our world with His gospel. We seek to help fulfil that by publishing books that point people towards Jesus and help them develop a Christ-like maturity. We aim to equip all levels of readers for life, work, ministry and mission.

Books in our adult range are published in three imprints.

Christian Focus contains popular works including biographies, commentaries, basic doctrine, and Christian living. Our children's books are also published in this imprint.

Mentor focuses on books written at a level suitable for Bible College and seminary students, pastors, and other serious readers; the imprint includes commentaries, doctrinal studies, examination of current issues, and church history.

Christian Heritage contains classic writings from the past.

For details of our titles visit us on our website
www.christianfocus.com

Christian Focus Publications Ltd
Geanies House, Fearn, Tain,
Ross-shire, IV20 ITW, Scotland, United Kingdom.
info@christianfocus.com

THE WORD WORLDWIDE

We first heard of WORD WORLDWIDE over twenty years ago when Marie Dinnen, its founder, shared excitedly about the wonderful way ministry to one needy woman had exploded to touch many lives. It was great to see the Word of God being made central in the lives of thousands of men and women, then to witness the life-changing results of them applying the Word to their circumstances. Over the years the vision for WORD WORLDWIDE has not dimmed in the hearts of those who are involved in this ministry. God is still at work through His Word and in today's self-seeking society, the Word is even more relevant to those who desire true meaning and purpose in life. WORD WORLDWIDE is a ministry of WEC International, an interdenominational missionary society, whose sole purpose is to see Christ known, loved and worshipped by all, particularly those who have yet to hear of His wonderful name. This ministry is a vital part of our work and we warmly recommend the WORD WORLDWIDE 'Geared for Growth' Bible studies to you. We know that as you study His Word you will be enriched in your personal walk with Christ. It is our hope that as you are blessed through these studies, you will find opportunities to help others discover a personal relationship with Jesus. As a mission we would encourage you to work with us to make Christ known to the ends of the earth.

Stewart and Jean Moulds – British Directors, **WEC International**.

A full list of over 50 'Geared for Growth' studies can be obtained from:

John and Ann Edwards
5 Louvaine Terrace, Hetton-le-Hole, Tyne & Wear, DH5 9PP
Tel. 0191 5262803 Email: rhysjohn.edwards@virgin.net

Anne Jenkins
2 Windermere Road, Carnforth, Lancs., LA5 9AR
Tel. 01524 734797 Email: anne@jenkins.abelgratis.com

UK Website: www.gearedforgrowth.co.uk